# A PIRATE

**Lincolnshire**
COUNTY COUNCIL

## discover libraries

**This book should be returned on or before
the due date.**

SEₐ 11.18

To renew or order library books please telephone 01522 782010
or visit https://lincolnshire.spydus.co.uk

You will require a Personal Identification Number.
Ask any member of staff for this.

**The above does not apply to Reader's Group Collection Stock.**

*Pirate Dad and Joe* ✳ CANNON

Ye be cordially invited to the

# BUCCANEERS' BALL

Chart ye course for Swashbuckler's Hall
at 7pm on Christmas Eve

## DON'T BE LATE!

# THE GREAT CHRISTMAS TREASURE HUNT

Here be treasure

Here be sharks

WATERFRONT

Ahoy there, mateys! Follow the map to find the TREASURE.
1st prize: GOLD and RUBIES! 2nd prize: Chocolate DOUBLOONS!
3rd prize: Tin of CUSTARD!

FOR DANIEL AND HIS PIRATE DAD   S.S

FOR CLARE, ANNA AND CHARLIE, WHO INSPIRE   A.C

Text copyright © 2018 Suzy Senior
Illustrations copyright © 2018 Andy Catling
This edition copyright © 2018 Lion Hudson IP Limited

Published by Lion Children's Books
an imprint of
**Lion Hudson Limited**
Wilkinson House, Jordan Hill Business Park,
Banbury Road, Oxford OX2 8DR, England
www.lionhudson.com/lionchildrens

ISBN 978 0 7459 7716 4

First edition 2018

A catalogue record for this book is available from the British Library

Printed and bound in Malaysia, April 2018, LH54

# A PIRATE CHRISTMAS

SUZY SENIOR  ANDY CATLING

LION
CHILDREN'S

The Buccaneers' Ball was in full swing!
Mouth-watering smells filled Swashbucklers' Hall.
The riotous singing was frightening the seagulls,
and the GREAT CHRISTMAS
TREASURE HUNT had just begun.

Across the water, Joe and Pirate Dad gazed glumly from the poop deck. Cannon, the ship's guinea pig, chewed miserably on a chunk of seaweed.

"I can't believe we're missing it," said Joe. "All our friends are there. It's the **best event** of the pirate year."

"Aye, lad," agreed Pirate Dad. "What a scurvy time for the
rowboat to spring a leak! Arrrr, well. How about I read us a nice
Christmas story?"
Joe grinned. A Christmassy story was sure to cheer them up –
all those presents and parties and snow.

Down in the captain's cabin, Pirate Dad opened a gigantic book. "Here! I've had this since I was a lad! Now, let's see…

"Many Years ago, in Nazareth, there was a lass named Mary. She was going to marry Joseph the carpenter. One day, an angel told Mary she would have a very special baby. Before the baby arrived Mary and Joseph had to go on a long journey to Bethlehem…"

"Alright!" said Joe. "I love voyages!"

"...on a donkey," continued Pirate Dad.

Joe looked less impressed, but Dad carried on:

"When Mary and Joseph arrived in Bethlehem, the town was full! The only place left to sleep was with the animals."

"Sounds a bit smelly," laughed Joe. Cannon gave Joe a hard guinea pig stare. She *always* shared a hammock with Joe, and he'd never complained before.

Pirate Dad read on:

"That night, Mary's baby was born.
She named him Jesus, and tucked him
up in the manger to sleep."

Cannon thought the baby looked
very comfortable in the soft hay. (She quite
liked babies... except when they cried. Then she just preferred hay.)

Eventually Pirate Dad managed to
turn the page:

"Out in the fields were some shepherds watching over
their sheep. Suddenly the sky was ablaze with light.
An angel appeared and told the shepherds about the baby.
They rushed off to find him!"

"This is a strange story, Dad," said Joe. "Where are all the presents and snow?"

"I'm not sure it's that kind of book," replied Pirate Dad, scratching his beard. He turned a few more pages…

# "Aharr! Here, my boy – this is a good bit!

"Wise men spied a new star in the skies. They journeyed from the east to look for a newborn king."

Joe looked puzzled.

"Never mind, lad! They brought **treasure!** Gold and frankincense (expensive stuff, that) and myrrh."

"Fantastic!" said Joe. "Christmas wouldn't be Christmas without treasure."

Pirate Dad grinned with a flash of a golden tooth, and turned the page.

"The Wise Men found the child and laid their gifts before him."

"Aha! Presents!" said Joe, looking relieved. "Strange presents for a baby, though."

"**Shiver me timbers**, everyone likes **GOLD**!" declared Pirate Dad. "It's the perfect gift."

"Anyway, look what it says here:

"*That little boy was God's own son;*
*His precious gift to all people.*"

"What?" asked Joe, really puzzled now.
"A gift? To *all people*? Even PIRATES?"
Pirate Dad turned the page to check!

"**Arrr**, lad, especially **pirates!** See, it says here,

"And he is the **greatest treasure** of all."

"Huh!" pondered Joe. "I like the sound of that."
"Aye. Me too, lad," said Pirate Dad and he
carefully closed the book.

Just then, a light flashed outside the porthole.
"Do you reckon it's angels?" grinned Joe, nudging Pirate Dad.

"Ahoy there!"

bellowed a piratey voice from close by.
"Probably not," said Pirate Dad.

They raced up to the deck and almost fell overboard in surprise! Clambering noisily aboard were all their pirate friends!

Barnacle Bob heaved barrels of juice.

Parakeet Pete carried pineapple rings.

Wesley O' West lugged boxes of biscuits.

"We missed you!" roared Pirate Dad's friend, **Lanky Sue.**

**"So we brought the party to you!"**

**Mantaray Mick** had a squeezebox and flute.

**Jellyfish Jean** brought banana ice cream.

**Matty McSeaweed** waved streamers and lanterns.

**Overboard Andy** brought coconut candy.

Very quickly, the party started up again. They ate, and sang, and danced for hours!

"Shame you missed the Great Christmas Treasure Hunt, though," said Lanky Sue.

Pirate Dad and Joe smiled at each other knowingly.
"Arrr, maybe so," said Pirate Dad with a cheerful wink.
"But Christmas treasure isn't always about gold."

When everyone had gone, Joe and Pirate Dad climbed into their hammocks and fell straight to sleep.

Outside, far above the ship, stars glittered in the clear night sky.

And soon it began to snow.

## Other Christmas titles from Lion Hudson

On That Christmas Night   *Lois Rock - Alison Jay*

Tales from Christmas Wood   *Suzy Senior – James Newman Gray*

The Animals' Christmas   *Elena Pasquali – Giuliano Ferri*

Countdown to Christmas   *Juliet David – Paul Nicholls*

The Midnight Visitors   *Juliet David – Jo Parry*

The Fox's Tale   *Nick Butterworth – Mick Inkpen*